The Father's Love

A bible study series with practical application to daily life.

Bible Study 3:

The Father's House

Luke Jeffery

The Father's Love

Onwards and Upwards Publications, Berkeley House,
11 Nightingale Crescent, West Horsley, Surrey KT24 6PD

www.onwardsandupwards.org

copyright © Luke Jeffery 2012

Scripture quotations taken from the HOLY BIBLE, NEW INTERNATIONAL VERSION. Copyright © 1973, 1978, 1984 by International Bible Society. Used by permission.

ISBN: 978-1-907509-47-6
Cover design: Leah-Maarit

Printed in the UK

Contents

About the Book Series

This eight-part book series 'The Father's Love' teaches how to experience the love of God concretely in your daily life. My aim is to open up the scriptures to you, one principle at a time, and to help you to see your own life from the perspective of God's Word. But I have also thrown in some stories, because we overcome Satan "by the blood of the lamb and the word of [our] testimony." Perhaps some of the stories from my life will give you the faith to apply the scriptures to your own life. Perhaps you can identify with my journey as I have struggled to understand the love of my heavenly Father in an imperfect world.

I strongly recommend that you read the series slowly. Each book contains a chapter at the end with tasks that will help you to apply the teaching to your daily life. After you have read each book, I suggest that you spend a week performing these tasks before moving on to the next topic.

The order of teaching in this series has been carefully chosen so that the teaching in the later books is built on principles laid down in the earlier books. That is why, to get the most out of the teaching, it is good to apply each principle before moving on. When you give yourself a week's break between each topic, it allows you to think through the truth more deeply and see how it applies to your life.

Introduction

In the first book of this series we learned that we have one true Father, our Father in Heaven. Fathers on earth were intended to demonstrate his nature and qualities, but this kind of fatherhood has never been seen. Instead, the Father reveals himself to us through the Word. By meditating on the truth and having our minds renewed, we can begin to experience his love in the way he intended.

The more we tell about his love, the more our faith increases. The more our faith increases, the more we experience. The more we experience, the more testimonies we have to tell.

In the second we learned about the nature of God's love and the meaning of the word 'checed'. We saw how checed becomes active exactly when we have reached the weakest possible point in life. Much more than simply mercy, it is a kind of love that bestows such favour upon us that the end result is better than if we had never faced the trial that got us there. It is a kindness that turns slaves and outcasts into kings and advisers.

We also learned that Jesus is the Word of God. He is a message from the Father. His whole life speaks of something that the Father wants us to know. In this book, we will dig a little deeper and find out what the Father's message is.

Story: God's Avatar

A few months ago, I went to watch the film 'Avatar' with a friend. It was the first time I have watched a modern 3D film and quite an exciting experience! But the movie itself left me with many thoughts about our relationship with God.

The story is set in the future. Humans want to gain access to a valuable resource on a planet inhabited by an alien race, but in order to do so they must communicate with that race. So they create an avatar, a creature that physically looks like one of the aliens but contains the mind of a human. The human lives through the creature and can live in the alien world, communicating with the local beings.

In a way, God has done the same thing in order to reach us. He created a body that we could see, communicate with and understand, and came to earth in the form of Jesus. Jesus himself chose to do only what he saw the Father doing. He listened to the Father's heart and thoughts and acted accordingly. In the film the motives of the humans were selfish. But the Father's motive in sending Jesus was entirely focused on our benefit. Through Jesus he wanted to reveal to us his love as a father and to make it possible to enter an intimate relationship with him that would last forever.

And so the Father lived and loved through Jesus. Jesus was also filled with the Holy Spirit, who led him from place to place. The whole deity of God was active on earth through the person of Christ, and people were able to see with human eyes what God is like.

For many people, avatar means a representation of a real person in a computer game or virtual world. When we "meet" people in an online game, we don't really physically meet them. Our avatar meets their avatar. But the avatar we create represents us and says what we tell it to say. In some games avatars have artificial intelligence and will make their own choices if we ask them to. But they always listen first to our commands.

This too is like Jesus' life on earth. He had a free will, but he submitted to the Father's will. In everything he listened and obeyed. Although he is God, and equal with the Father, he humbled himself and allowed the Father to live and work through him. He was even willing to die on a cross and carry our sins because it was the Father's will.

The original word 'avatar' comes from Hinduism. It means the deliberate manifestation of a deity on the earth. It is, however, incredible to think that the One True Deity did far more than manifest himself. He actually shared our physical life, becoming fully human. He experienced our trials, temptations and suffering. It was not easier for him than for any other man on earth. And yet he lived his life without sin.

Let that profound thought sink in as we look together at the life and message of Jesus.

Knowing the Father

John 1:1-4

In the beginning was the Word, and the Word was with God, and the Word was God. He was with God in the beginning. <u>Through him all things were made;</u> without him nothing was made that has been made. In him was life, and <u>that life was the light of men.</u>

Jesus was with the Father right at the very beginning. The account of creation in Genesis tells us that everything was created through God's words. He said, "Let there be light," and light was created. But here we are told that Jesus is the Word of God through whom everything was created.

Everything that Jesus created was according to the words of the Father, according to what flowed from the Father's heart.

Luke 6:45

The good man brings good things out of the good stored up in his heart, and the evil man brings evil things out of the evil stored up in his heart. For <u>out of the overflow of his heart his mouth speaks.</u>

In the second book of this series, we learned that the whole universe tells us something about the Father. His creation is intended to reveal who he is. We too are intended to reveal who he is.

Jesus brought life into the world, according to the Father's plan. And this doesn't mean just physical life. We are told that "that life was the light of men." Light reveals things that are hidden by darkness. It exposes things and allows us to see clearly.

Jesus came to reveal something.

John 1:9-13

<u>The true light that gives light</u> to every man was coming into the world. He was in the world, and though the world was made through him, the world did not recognize him. He came to that which was his own, but his own did not receive him. Yet to all who received him, to those who believed in his name, he gave <u>the right to become children of God</u> - children born not of natural descent, nor of human decision or a husband's will, but born of God.

Jesus, the giver of light, came into the world. And what he gave people was... the right to become children of God. Jesus came to restore our relationship with the Father. As believers, we know that the blood of Jesus was shed so that we could be forgiven of the sin that separates us from the Father. We know that his death on the cross made it possible for us to be reunited with God. But Jesus' ministry included more than just his death and resurrection. His whole life revealed a message from the Father that reached its climax in his death.

John 1:18

No one has ever seen God, but God the One and Only, who is at the Father's side, has <u>made him known</u>.

The purpose of Jesus' life was to make the Father known. The Father's message to mankind was, "Look! This is who I am!"

We see this hinted in one of the most well-known verses of the Bible.

John 14:6

Jesus answered, "I am the way and the truth and <u>the life</u>. No one comes to <u>the Father</u> except through me."

We already read that there is life in Jesus. It is the kind of life that reveals things that are hidden. It is the kind of life that carries a message. In Jesus there is life that makes the Father known.

Now Jesus says, "I *am* the life." He *is* the light. He *is* the message. And he adds, "No one comes to the Father except through me." He is the only one who can reveal who the Father is. He is the only one who can make it possible to know the Father.

But let's read this verse in its proper context.

The Father's House

John 14:1-4

Do not let your hearts be troubled. Trust in God; trust also in me. <u>In my Father's house are many rooms</u>; if it were not so, I would have told you. <u>I am going there to prepare a place for you.</u> And if I go and prepare a place for you, I will come back and take you to be with me that you also may be where I am.

What an announcement! Jesus talks about the Father's house – the place where the Father lives. He tells his disciples that the Father has a big house; he intends for a lot of people to live there. And Jesus promises to go and make a place ready for each of the disciples. Each one has a promise to live close to the Father, under his care. Not only that, but Jesus is going to personally take them there.

What does it mean to live in your father's house? It means that you have a safe home to dwell in. It means that the father looks after all those living in his house. It means that you will get meals on the table. It means you will be provided for. But most importantly, it means that you are *part of a family* and can enjoy a relationship with the family and with the father who leads the family.

And so, Jesus says, "The Father wants a relationship with you. He wants to be your Father. He wants to protect you, provide for you, and pour out his love upon you. He wants to spend time with you and he wants you to become part of a loving family."

John 14:4-6

"You know the way to the place where I am going." Thomas said to him, "Lord, we don't know where you are going, so how can we know the way?" Jesus answered, "<u>I am the way</u> and the truth and the life. No one comes to the Father except through me."

The disciples don't understand. They don't know where the Father's house is, let alone how to get there. But Jesus explains. He is the way. By his death, he is going to give each person a right to become a child of God and live in the house of the Father. God's house has many rooms because it was made for many people. Through Jesus we have a way to enter God's house.

And that is why Jesus says, "Do not let your hearts be troubled." We have nothing of any real consequence to worry about. We have the right to spend eternity in the house of the Father, enjoying his love and presence forever!

The Father revealed

John 14:6-7

Jesus answered, "I am the way and the truth and the life. No one comes to the Father except through me. If you really knew me, you would know my Father as well. From now on, you do know him and have seen him."

Jesus goes on to reveal the message. He has come to make the Father known. Anyone who knows him, knows the Father. He is the full revelation of who the Father is. But still the disciples don't understand. They want to *see* the Father.

John 14:8-9

Philip said, "Lord, show us the Father and that will be enough for us." Jesus answered: "Don't you know me, Philip, even after I have been among you such a long time? Anyone who has seen me has seen the Father. How can you say, 'Show us the Father'?"

Jesus' answer is direct. Anyone who has seen him has seen the Father. In Jesus, the Fatherhood of God is fully revealed.

John 14:10

Don't you believe that I am in the Father, and that the Father is in me? The words I say to you are not just *my own. Rather, <u>it is the Father, living in me, who is doing his work</u>.*

As we listen to the words of Jesus and follow his life, we will learn what true fatherhood is. Just as in the act of creation, everything that Jesus does is according to what is on the Father's heart. As we watch him, we see the Father in action. As we listen to him, we understand the truth of the Father's love.

John 5:19-20

Jesus gave them this answer: "I tell you the truth, the Son can do nothing by himself; he can do only what he <u>sees his Father doing</u>, because whatever the Father does the Son also does. For the Father loves the Son and <u>shows him all he does</u>. Yes, to your amazement he will show him even greater things than these."

John 6:45-47

It is written in the Prophets: 'They will all be taught by God.' Everyone who listens to the Father and learns from him comes to me. No one has seen the Father except the one who is from God; only he has <u>seen the Father</u>. I tell you the truth, he who believes has everlasting life.

Jesus' actions were the Father's actions. He simply did what he saw the Father doing - no more, no less. And so, through Jesus, the Father taught the people.

But what does Jesus mean when he says that "he who believes" will have "everlasting life"? It cannot just mean living forever, because Jesus teaches that all people will live forever.

Matthew 25:41-46

Then he will say to those on his left, 'Depart from me, you who are cursed, into the eternal fire prepared for the devil and his angels. For I was hungry and you gave me nothing to eat, I was thirsty and you gave me nothing to drink, I was a stranger and you did not invite me in, I needed clothes and you did not clothe me, I was sick and in prison and you did not look after me.' They also will answer, 'Lord, when did we see you hungry or thirsty or a stranger or needing clothes or sick or in prison, and did not help you?' He will reply, 'I tell you the truth, whatever you did not do for one of the least of these, you did not do for me.' <u>Then they will go away to eternal punishment, but the righteous to eternal life</u>.

There is a distinction between eternal punishment and eternal life. So, the eternal life is the very life that Jesus came to bring. Its secret is in the message that he carries. And the secret is revealed in the well-known passage John 3:16.

John 3:16

For God so <u>loved the world</u> that he gave his one and only Son, that whoever believes in him shall not perish but have eternal life.

It is the Father's love that prompts him to send his Son, Jesus. Through Jesus, he reveals his love. And whoever believes in him, in the Word of God, in the message of the Father's love, will live forever in that love.

The Father's house has a room for you too. The Father wants to pour out his love and favour upon you.

As you hear the message, believe it in your heart, and you will begin to live in the love that the Father has for you.

Eternal inheritance

We now understand that Jesus came to reveal to us the Father, and to make it possible for us to have the relationship with the Father that was intended from the very beginning. He wants us to experience 'True Fatherhood', and so his life demonstrates to us what the Father is like.

Now let us look in more detail at some of the things Jesus teaches about the Father and the inheritance he has prepared for us.

Luke 15:11-12

Jesus continued: "There was <u>a man who had two sons</u>. The younger one said to his father, 'Father, give me my share of the estate.' So he divided his property between them."

In this passage, Jesus begins to tell a story to illustrate the relationship between The Father and us, his sons. The Father is rich and owns an estate. That estate will one day belong to the sons, but for now they simply live in the Father's house.

The Bible tells very much about the fact that the Father has a great inheritance for us that will be ours to enjoy forever in heaven. There are too many examples to cover in detail here, but we shall look at a few.

Hebrews 9:15

For this reason Christ is the mediator of a new covenant, that those who are called may <u>receive the promised eternal inheritance</u> - now that he has died as a ransom to set them free from the sins committed under the first covenant.

We have seen that Jesus' death enables us to enter the Father's house. His death also enables us to receive the inheritance that the Father has prepared for us. Now we live in his house, but he is planning to give everything he owns to us to enjoy.

Matthew 25:34

Then the King will say to those on his right, 'Come, you who are blessed by my Father; take <u>your inheritance, the kingdom prepared for you</u> since the creation of the world.'

The Kingdom belongs to God. That is why we pray "yours is the Kingdom". According to scripture, Jesus will one day hand the whole Kingdom over to the Father.

1 Corinthians 15:24

Then the end will come, when he <u>hands over the kingdom to God the Father</u> after he has destroyed all dominion, authority and power.

But, amazingly, the Kingdom has been prepared for *us*. He owns the estate, but he is saving it as an inheritance for us.

1 Peter 1:3-5

Praise be to the God and Father of our Lord Jesus Christ! In his great mercy he has given us new birth into a living hope through the resurrection of Jesus Christ from the dead, and into <u>an inheritance</u> that can never perish, spoil or fade - <u>kept in heaven for you</u>, who through faith are shielded by God's power until the coming of the salvation that is ready to be revealed in the last time.

Ephesians 1:18-19

I pray also that <u>the eyes of your heart may be enlightened</u> in order that you may know the hope to which he has called you, the riches of <u>his glorious inheritance</u> in the saints, and his incomparably great power for us who believe.

We don't even know yet what the inheritance will look like. It is being stored away for us and will only be revealed when Jesus returns and God judges the world. But we can be sure of one thing – it will be infinitely better than gaining a grand estate here on earth. Our Father owns everything and he is a generous Father. What he has prepared for us is worth waiting for.

It is hard to picture something we have never seen. But we need to pray for a revelation of the inheritance. We need to continually set our mind on heavenly things. We need to dream about it and live for it, even though we do not know what it will be.

Ephesians 1:13-15

And you also were included in Christ when you heard the word of truth, the gospel of your salvation. Having believed, you were marked in him with a seal, the promised <u>Holy Spirit, who is a deposit guaranteeing our inheritance</u> until the redemption of those who are God's possession - to the praise of his glory.

We have seen that the only things that will last in heaven are things that God does. Our inheritance and reward will only be received if what we have done survives the Day of Judgement. But we can have confidence if we are filled with the Holy Spirit. He himself builds things through our lives that last forever.

Parable: The Sad Father

I once knew a father with a teenage son. The father wanted to spend quality time with the son, but the son had his own friends and his own life. Whenever the father suggested a hobby that they could do together, the son was not interested. Sometimes the father felt he needed to give his son some advice or direction, but the son was always too tired to listen.

The father tried to understand his son's life, but the distance between them seemed to grow rapidly as time passed. The son would often spend whole nights away with his friends, but would sometimes return in the early hours of the morning. He never told his plans in advance – the father always left the lights on in the hallway, just in case.

In fact, there was only one kind of occasion on which the son would spend time with his father. He would come into the room and have a brief chat. In those moments he would be willing to talk about almost anything. But the conversation quickly came around to the main point. He needed money to buy more petrol for his motorbike. Or, his friends were going out for a meal, but he was broke. Or, maybe he wanted to go to the cinema and needed cash to buy a ticket.

Whenever the son came to have a chat, the father knew that the conversation would soon turn to a request for money. The father gave the money. But inside he felt very saddened, even hurt. His son was just using him, and was not interested in relationship.

His son was also missing the very best – the father had so much more to give than money...

I want my inheritance now!

Let us return to the story that Jesus was telling about the father and sons. Of the two sons, one of them wanted his inheritance now. He said, "Father, give me my share of the estate."

Jesus tells us more about people like this.

Matthew 6:1

Be careful not to do your 'acts of righteousness' before men, to be seen by them. If you do, you will have <u>no reward</u> from your Father in heaven.

Some people want their reward now; so they do good things, inspired by God, but they do them in such a way that they will be noticed. They perhaps want to receive honour and recognition. They perhaps want people to praise them and maybe give them a more significant role in the community. They perhaps want to receive money for their work.

How about you? What are your motives for the good deeds that you do? Do you hope that someone will notice and encourage you? Do you hope that your church will recognize your good work and give you more responsibility? Are you giving in order to get something back? What is your agenda?

Here are some practical examples:

Matthew 6:2-4

So when you give to the needy, do not announce it with trumpets, as the hypocrites do in the synagogues and on the streets, <u>to be honored by men</u>. I tell you the truth, <u>they have received their reward</u> in full. But when you give to the needy, do not let your left hand know what your right hand is doing, so that your giving may be in secret. Then <u>your Father, who sees what is done in secret, will reward you</u>.

Matthew 6:5-6

And when you pray, do not be like the hypocrites, for they love to pray standing in the synagogues and on the street corners <u>to be seen by men</u>. I tell you the truth, <u>they have received their reward</u> in full. But when you pray, go into your room, close the door and pray to your Father, who is unseen. Then <u>your Father, who sees what is done in secret, will reward you</u>.

Matthew 6:16-18

When you fast, do not look somber as the hypocrites do, for they disfigure their faces <u>to show men</u> they are fasting. I tell you the truth, <u>they have received their reward</u> in full. But when you fast, put oil on your head and wash your face, so that it will not be obvious to men that you are fasting, but only to your Father, who is unseen; and <u>your Father, who sees what is done in secret, will reward you</u>.

Let's see what happens to the son in Jesus' story who wants his inheritance immediately.

Luke 15:13-14

Not long after that, the younger son got together all he had, <u>set off for a distant country</u> and there squandered his wealth in wild living. After he had spent everything, there was a severe famine in that whole country, and <u>he began to be in need</u>.

How tragic! Here we have a born-again Christian, brought into the house of the Father, and filled with the Spirit of God. He has been blessed with love, with joy and with peace. He has the right to live as a son, and he has the right to half of everything the Father owns. He is blessed and rich. But with all those riches... he leaves the house!

He has the blessings of the Father, but he does not want to actually live in a relationship with the Father. Nor does the Father take the inheritance back. It has already been given to the son. He can squander it now or he can enjoy it later. The gift is already given.

We have the same choice. We can squander the blessings of the Father now or we can wait to receive an inheritance that will last forever.

See what the son does. He goes to a distant country. We have learned that we are citizens of heaven. Here on earth we are foreigners. But where do we really choose to live? Do we want to live in our Father's house, enjoy his presence and wait for the inheritance? Or do we want to live for this short time here on earth, enjoying all the "blessings" here?

Like the son in the story, if we receive our reward now we will soon find that it does not last. It is not an eternal reward. All those who live for this world will eventually experience a time of "severe famine". Every pleasure on earth is coming to an end. Only the things that last forever in heaven will count.

Jesus warns about this with very strong words.

Luke 6:24-26

But woe to you who are rich, for <u>you have already received your comfort</u>. Woe to you who are well fed now, for you will go hungry. Woe to you who laugh now, for you will mourn and weep. Woe to you when all men speak well of you, for that is how their fathers treated the false prophets.

But he has another message for those who choose to forego their reward now and wait for an inheritance in heaven.

Luke 6:20-23

Looking at his disciples, he said: "Blessed are you who are poor, for <u>yours is the kingdom of God</u>. Blessed are you who hunger now, for you will be satisfied. Blessed are you who weep now, for you will laugh. Blessed are you when men hate you, when they exclude you and insult you and reject your name as evil, because of the Son of Man. Rejoice in that day and leap for joy, because <u>great is your reward in heaven</u>. For that is how their fathers treated the prophets."

Now let's see what happens to the son who lived for his reward on earth.

Luke 15:15-16

So he went and <u>hired himself out</u> to a citizen of that country, who sent him to his fields to feed pigs. He longed to fill his stomach with the pods that the pigs were eating, but no one gave him anything.

He has lived for the world and its pleasures, and eventually he becomes a slave to the world. Although he is still a legal son of the rich father, he becomes an abused servant of a citizen in the foreign country. He has completely lost all sense of identity. He does not know any more who he is. He seems to have lost the Father's blessing. He is distant from the Father and does not enjoy his presence or favour. His own sins and wrong decisions haunt him. He knows he has backslidden, and there seems to be no way back any more.

And then, something changes...

Return to the Father's House

Luke 15:17-19

When he <u>came to his senses</u>, he said, 'How many of my father's hired men have food to spare, and here I am starving to death! I will set out and <u>go back to my father</u> and say to him: Father, I have sinned against heaven and against you. I am no longer worthy to be called your son; make me like one of your hired men.'

For all intents and purposes he has reached the end of his life. There is no inheritance waiting for him anymore. He knows that he has not lived in relationship with his Father and no longer feels that he is worthy to be called a son. He knows that he was never really interested in the Father – only in what he could *get* from the Father. But he comes to the point of confessing his sin. And for the first time he shows a small sign of faith – maybe the Father would receive him back as a servant.

How about you? Have you been living for this world and what you can get out of it? Is the purpose of your life really to live in relationship with the Father, or are you mainly concerned with what he can do for you? Don't wait until the famine before you wake up to the truth. Life is short!

You may feel that you have already gone past the point of no return. God could never accept you back as a son. Maybe you feel that you have committed a sin that cannot be forgiven. Maybe you know that you have already wasted your life and squandered the inheritance. But like this son, are you ready to have faith in just one thing? Can you have faith in the fact that God is a good and loving Father? Let's see what God says about himself, when he tells Moses who he is:

Exodus 34:5-7
Then the LORD came down in the cloud and stood there with him and proclaimed his name, the LORD. And he passed in front of Moses, proclaiming, "The LORD, the LORD, the compassionate and gracious God, <u>slow to anger, abounding in love</u> and faithfulness, <u>maintaining</u> **checed** *to thousands, and <u>forgiving wickedness, rebellion and sin</u>. Yet he does not leave the guilty unpunished; he punishes the children and their children for the sin of the fathers to the third and fourth generation.*

Can you believe, as the son did, that the Father has "maintained checed" towards you? Can you believe that he might forgive your rebellion and sin? Can you believe that he is compassionate? Can you believe that he is gracious, and might just allow you to serve him again? Can you believe that he is so slow to anger that he is still waiting for you to return to him?

Luke 15:20-24
So he got up and went to his father. "But while he was still a long way off, <u>his father saw him and was filled with compassion</u> for him; <u>he ran to his son, threw his arms around him and kissed him</u>. The son said to him, 'Father, I have sinned against heaven and against you.

> *I am no longer worthy to be called your son.' But the father said to his servants, 'Quick! Bring the best robe and put it on him. Put a ring on his finger and sandals on his feet. Bring the fattened calf and kill it. <u>Let's have a feast and celebrate</u>. For this son of mine was dead and is alive again; he was lost and is found.' So they began to celebrate.*

Now we see what the True Father is really like. There is no inheritance to give any more, and the son has thoroughly wasted his life and squandered everything. But that was never really the point. It was never really about riches, not even riches in heaven. It was about the fact that Father wanted to have a living relationship with the son. The Father wanted to pour his love out on the son. He poured his love out with an inheritance, but the inheritance was just a demonstration of that love. The Father's love did not change just because the inheritance was wasted.

If you are not living in the Father's house, he is waiting for you too. In fact, as soon as he sees the first sign that you are willing to return to him, he will run to you and put his arms around you. You don't have to earn your way back to him. He doesn't want you as a servant. He wants you as a son. He is filled with compassion towards you.

And see what the Father does. He gives a ring – a sign of honour and authority. He gives sandals – giving you comfort and taking care of your needs. And he kills the fattened calf. He gives you the very best that he has. The fattened calf is not killed for just anyone. You will be received with great honour.

This is unfailing checed in action!

That is why when believers return to the Father they often experience him in a powerful and concrete way. They see his love streaming through their lives. They are filled with joy. They often seem even more blessed than faithful believers who follow the Lord day by day.

Checed can be overwhelming. The Father's love is beyond measure.

Will you turn back to him today? All you have to do is approach him in prayer. Tell him you want to come back to live in his house. And begin a new relationship with him. Leave your earthly agenda behind, and plan eternity with the Father.

But there is more to this story. Let's see how the other son reacts.

Luke 15:25-30

Meanwhile, the older son was in the field. When he came near the house, he heard music and dancing. So he called one of the servants and asked him what was going on. 'Your brother has come,' he replied, 'and your father has killed the fattened calf because he has him back safe and sound.' <u>The older brother became angry</u> and refused to go in. So his father went out and pleaded with him. But he answered his father, 'Look! All these years I've been slaving for you and never disobeyed your orders. Yet you never gave me even a young goat so I could celebrate with my friends. But when this son of yours who has squandered your property with *prostitutes comes home, you kill the fattened calf for him!'*

We might think that the older son has had a revelation of the Father's love. He has remained in the Father's presence, and he has saved up his inheritance. He has obeyed the teachings of Jesus – he has not tried to gain reputation or wealth here on earth. He has obeyed every command that the Father has given, and he has lived wisely.

But now he gets angry. He has lived in the Father's house all this time, but the son who rejected the Father has been given greater honour than he has. The older son has worked hard for his eternal inheritance and has not been disturbed by the fact that his younger brother was living a life of ease. He knew that one day his younger brother's inheritance would run out, but his inheritance with the Father would last forever. He has kept his mind on things above whilst his younger brother has been thinking about earthly things.

But now his younger brother has come back, and the Father he has worked for has honoured his younger brother in his own house. It just seems so unfair.

The Value of the Father's Presence

Let's see how the Father responds.

Luke 15:31-32

'My son,' the father said, 'you are always with me, and everything I have is yours. But we had to celebrate and be glad, because this brother of yours was dead and is alive again; he was lost and is found.'

It seems that the older brother did not really understand the Father's love after all. He was trying to earn the Father's approval with his good works. He was certainly living wisely and earning an eternal reward, but although he lived in the Father's house, he was not enjoying the Father's love.

The Father responds in two ways.

Firstly, "You are always with me." The older son had not understood what was really important. The fattened calf wasn't the point of living in the Father's house. The older son had been able to enjoy something far more precious than a feast – the presence of the Father himself. When we remain in the Father's house we have his protection and provision but, best of all, we have the Father himself.

When we have a revelation of the value of just *being* with the Father, we will not feel offended when somebody else returns to the Father and is shown checed. We will be happy that they too can finally enjoy his presence. The older son had not understood that being with the Father

33

was a far better life than all the "pleasures" that the younger son had "enjoyed". The older son had had the better deal all along, but he had been blind to it and had not enjoyed it.

The second thing that the Father said to the older son was "Everything I have is yours."

The older son could have enjoyed anything in his Father's house at any time. If only he had believed in the Father's generosity, he could have asked for the fattened calf and eaten it with his own friends. The Father would have been willing to give anything.

It is the same with us when we live in the Father's house. Everything he has is ours. But often we think that we have to earn his blessing and his favour with our actions. Then, if we see that he blesses someone who has not even lived righteously, we are offended.

Do you remember what we learned about offence? We can become offended by the Father, but the sin is on our side. If we really understood the Father's love, we would not become offended. The older son did not have a complete understanding. He did not realize that the Father is primarily interested in relationship, not in what we can do for him.

This does not mean that we should not work hard for the Father.

Colossians 3:23-24

Whatever you do, <u>work at it with all your heart</u>, as working for the Lord, not for men, since you know that

> *you will receive an inheritance from the Lord as a reward. It is the Lord Christ you are serving.*

By working hard for him, we store up a reward for ourselves. And the older son was wise to work hard and guard his inheritance. He was wise to save his inheritance until later.

However, we should also understand that the love of the Father is unconditional.

Testimony: As a Doorkeeper

After the Father first called me into youth ministry, it was a little while before I was invited to participate in youth meetings. For many months I was praying for the youth in our church, trying to get to know as much about them as possible and looking for ways to be involved.

I was eager to teach the youth, to lead worship and to serve in prayer ministry. But most of all, I just wanted to hang out with them and be their friend. I believed that through friendship I could really get to know young people well enough to pray effectively for them and encourage them forward in their gifting.

Eventually, I decided to take a more proactive approach so I wrote an email to the local youth worker and expressed my desire to serve at the youth meeting. I said that I would be willing to do whatever needed to be done.

Before long I received a phone call. "It would be great if you could serve on the door and make sure that only youth come into the meeting."

Inside my heart, I was shouting, "NOOOOO!" It really wasn't what I wanted to do. I wanted to be in the main hall with the youth. But God had instructed me to serve in any way I was asked.

So I replied, "Yes, of course. I would love to."

The next week, I decided to try again. I wrote another email offering any help that would be needed. And the same reply came back: "It would be great if you could serve on the door." I endured it, but as soon as my shift was over, I pretty much *ran* into the youth meeting, full of energy and enthusiasm. Even if I could not attend the meetings, I could at least spend the later part of the evenings with the youth.

Then it happened a third time.

I stood at the door, taking the opportunity to at least share a few words with teenagers as they came to the meeting. Outwardly, I was smiling and peaceful. But inside I was frustrated. I began to talk to the Father about it.

"Lord, I feel sure you have called me to do more than this. I don't feel that the door is my place or my calling. I long to be in the meetings and to spend time with the youth. But you have asked me to serve you wherever I am placed so I cannot complain. Still, Lord, my prayer is that you would make the youth worker aware that this is not really what is on my heart."

I heard the Father laughing, and he reminded me of the words of Psalm 84:10: "I would rather be a doorkeeper in the house of my God than dwell in the tents of the wicked."

He said, "When you were younger you used to pray those words every day. You told me that you would rather be a doorkeeper in my house. Well... I just wanted to find out if it is true!"

I replied, "Well, Father, deep in my heart it *is* true. I *would* rather be here at the door than "living it up" in the world. It is better to be the lowest servant in the church than to live a life of meaningless luxury outside. And if this is your place for me, that is really fine. But if I have a choice of being a doorkeeper in your house or doing something else in your house, I feel quite ready to move away from the door!"

The Father laughed again and said, "Don't worry. You won't be here forever. Your day is coming."

That might have even been my last time on the door. All I remember is that before long I was serving in many other ways, and I was able to build friendships with the youth and young adults that had been on my heart for so long. And now, as a youth worker myself, I have begun to understand that the doorkeeper's work is one of the most important tasks there is. The safety and wellbeing of the youth is absolutely critical. I didn't realize it back then, but I had actually been honoured with a really valuable ministry. By standing at my post, I was enabling the work of the Kingdom to move forward safely.

One thing remained very clear to me after this little experience – the most important thing is to remain in the house of God. There you find joy, peace, hope, fellowship with the family of God and, best of all, the wonderful presence of the Father himself.

Tents on Earth. Home in Heaven.

It is so easy to get caught up with the cares and problems of this life. Even those of us who live in the richest countries of the world easily find ourselves worrying about the place that we live.

It is not wrong to live in a comfortable house and to build a safe environment to live in. But so easily our lives can be distracted from storing up treasures in heaven and our mission on earth by problems as mundane as a washing machine breaking down.

We invest long hours into paid work in order to pay the mortgage and buy more things for our home. Then we work more hours to keep everything secure and in good condition. We work even more to pay out for insurance, and then invest time making insurance claims.

I repeat – it is not wrong to live in a comfortable house. You can invest time in your home in order to use it for the Kingdom of Heaven. You can show hospitality and store up treasures in heaven. You can create a peaceful, joyful environment to invite people to and share the love of God.

Of course the Father wants you to have a safe place to dwell and to enjoy your home. But he doesn't want you to become a slave to your home. When your home stops you from enjoying a fulfilling relationship with God, something has fallen out of balance.

When you have a full revelation of the 'House of God', you will never again worry about your home or even where you will live. Whatever God calls you to do, you will trust him to provide all you need.

Jesus had this kind of trust. At times he was without a place to spend the night.

Matthew 8:19-20

Then a teacher of the law came to him and said, "Teacher, I will follow you wherever you go." Jesus replied, "Foxes have holes and birds of the air have nests, but <u>the Son of Man has no place to lay his head</u>."

And yet, we find him peacefully sleeping in a boat, trusting completely in the love of his Father.

Matthew 8:23-26

Then he got into the boat and his disciples followed him. Without warning, <u>a furious storm came up on the lake</u>, so that the waves swept over the boat. <u>But Jesus was sleeping</u>. The disciples went and woke him, saying, "Lord, save us! We're going to drown!" He replied, "You of little faith, why are you so afraid?" Then he got up and rebuked the winds and the waves, and it was completely calm.

Paul also experienced being without a home.

1 Corinthians 4:11

To this very hour we go hungry and thirsty, we are in rags, we are brutally treated, <u>we are homeless</u>.

But both had a great revelation of their home in heaven. Jesus, who had seen the Father's house, considered a house on earth to be nothing in comparison. Neither considered their homelessness to be a problem because they understood the Father's love. They knew that a home awaited in heaven that would last for eternity.

Abraham also experienced a kind of earthly homelessness.

Hebrews 11:8-10

By faith Abraham, when called to go to a place he would later receive as his inheritance, obeyed and went, even though he did not know where he was going. By faith he made his home in the promised land like a stranger in a foreign country; he lived in tents, as did Isaac and Jacob, who were heirs with him of the same promise. For he was looking forward to the city with foundations, whose architect and builder is God.

Abraham wandered around, living in tents. But he had a revelation of his future home in heaven. He believed in the love of the Father. He waited for the time when he would enter his Father's house and receive his inheritance.

In fact, Hebrews 11 tells that this attitude is a hallmark of all those who live by faith.

Hebrews 11:13-16

All these people were still living by faith when they died. They did not receive the things promised; they only saw them and welcomed them from a distance. And

41

> *they admitted that they were aliens and strangers on earth. People who say such things show that they are looking for a country of their own. If they had been thinking of the country they had left, they would have had opportunity to return. Instead, they were longing for a better country - a heavenly one. Therefore God is not ashamed to be called their God, for he has prepared a city for them.*

An earthly home is a good thing – a blessing from God. But we should not allow our earthly home to distract us from our heavenly home. If your eyes are fixed on your heavenly home, you will not worry. You won't worry where the rent money will come from. You won't worry about your household. You *will* be responsible. You *will* be hard-working. *But you won't worry!* You will recognize that the Father knows your needs and you will expect to see him take care of you.

Fulfilled in God's House

We have seen that David had a revelation of the Father's heart. In his life he reached the lowest rung of society, yet God made him King over all Israel. Let's see what David writes about the house of God.

Psalm 52:8

*But I am like an olive tree <u>flourishing in the house of God</u>; I trust in God's <u>unfailing</u> **checed** for ever and ever.*

He wrote this at a time when he had no home and King Saul was trying to kill him. And yet he sees himself as living in God's house, and doing well there! Here is another.

Psalm 84

How lovely is your <u>dwelling place</u>, O LORD Almighty! My soul yearns, even faints, for the courts of the LORD; <u>my heart and my flesh cry out for the living God</u>. Even the sparrow has found <u>a home</u>, and the swallow a nest for herself, where she may have her young - a place near your altar, O LORD Almighty, my King and my God. Blessed are <u>those who dwell in your house</u>; they <u>are ever praising you. Selah</u>

The last word, selah, is a musical term meaning "pause for a moment and let that thought sink in."

Those who live in God's house are always praising him. They are always full of joy. It doesn't matter whether they live in an earthly palace or are homeless. They are still happy! They are blessed! Pause for a moment and let that thought sink in!

David realizes that there is nothing on earth that can satisfy him. Only the "courts of the Lord" fulfil him. David is one of those who understand that the best thing about the house of God is that the Father lives there. "My heart and my flesh cry out for the living God."

Psalm 84:10

Better is one day in your courts than a thousand elsewhere; <u>I would rather be a doorkeeper in the house of my God</u> than dwell in the tents of the wicked.

There is no better place to be than in the house of God. Even being a servant there is better than living anywhere else!

Psalm 92:12-13

The righteous will <u>flourish like a palm tree</u>, they will grow like a cedar of Lebanon; <u>planted in the house of the LORD</u>, they will flourish in the courts of our God.

Let me state it again – a comfortable home on earth is a blessing. I am not suggesting that everyone should sell their homes and live on the streets. And the Father knows that we need a roof over our heads. He knows that we will die if we don't eat or drink or if we get too cold or too hot.

Matthew 6:31-33

So do not worry, saying, 'What shall we eat?' or 'What shall we drink?' or 'What shall we wear?' For the pagans run after all these things, and <u>your heavenly Father knows that you need them</u>. But seek first his kingdom and his righteousness, and all these things will be given to you as well.

This speaks of food, drink and clothes, but the principle is the same: the Father will take care of our needs. Our focus must be on things of heaven. We can be sure he will take care of these other things.

We cannot take our earthly home to heaven. Solomon said that everything is meaningless. That includes our home. In the context of eternity it is nothing more than a breath. It is zero. So if your need for a home distracts you from storing up treasure in heaven, you are in danger of losing the wonderful, eternal gifts that the Father wants to lavish upon you.

Conclusion

David sums up everything we have learned in psalm 36.

Psalm 36:5-9

Your __checed__, O LORD, reaches to the heavens, your faithfulness to the skies. Your righteousness is like the mighty mountains, your justice like the great deep. O LORD, you preserve both man and beast. How priceless is your unfailing __checed__! Both high and low among men find refuge in the shadow of your wings. They feast on the abundance of your house; you give them drink from your river of delights. For with you is the fountain of life; in your light we see light.

Jesus "is the fountain of life. In his light we see light."

As we have seen, the life that Jesus brings is eternal life in the house of the Father. It is the presence of God and a place in a family. It is all about relationship with the Father and with our brothers and sisters. As a light, Jesus reveals to us who the Father is, what he is like, and teaches us about the Father's house.

It's all about the Father's love. When we are with him, we find true fulfilment, true safety and true happiness. We can live under the shadow of his wings (under his protection) every day, now and in heaven.

We have already entered the Father's house. When we repented of our sins and confessed Jesus as our Lord and saviour, we became sons of the Father, welcomed into his home. In the books of this series that follow, we will continue to learn how to remain there and how to be sure of the inheritance that will last forever.

Action!

Memory verse

Memorise the following verse and try to keep it memorised also after the course has been completed.

Luke 15:31-32

'My son,' the father said, 'you are always with me, and everything I have is yours. But we had to celebrate and be glad, because this brother of yours was dead and is alive again; he was lost and is found.'

This verse will help you to keep in mind what is really important and to tap into the good things that the Father wants to give you.

The Younger Son

Reflect for a while on the parable of the Father and the two sons.

The first son received an inheritance from the Father but wanted his reward immediately.

How has God blessed your life?

- Do you have family and friends? Do you have a spouse or children?
- Do you have a home? Do you have furniture? A car? Other material possessions?

- Do you have opportunities to serve? Are there people around you with needs that you can meet?
- Do you have time to relax and enjoy life? Do you have money to spend on something above and beyond your basic needs? Do you have a job?
- Do you have opportunities for justice - to get your own back on those who have treated you unfairly?

Now think about how you use those blessings. To what extent do you receive your reward now, and to what extent do you save your reward for heaven?

You might want to look at the following verses which teach some of the ways to use our blessings here on earth to receive a reward in heaven. There are others too!

- **Hebrews 11:6** – Passion for God
- **Matthew 10:40-42** – Love for the body of Christ
- **1 Timothy 6:17-19; Proverbs 19:17** – Love for the poor
- **Matthew 25:31-40** – Love for those rejected by society
- **Proverbs 25:21-22; Matthew 5:44-47; Luke 6:35** – Love for your enemies
- **1 Corinthians 9:20-25** – Love for the world

Ask the Holy Spirit to show you any areas in which you are squandering your inheritance here on earth. Bring these things to the Father in confession, and thank him for the eternal reward that he wants to give you in heaven.

Here is an example prayer of confession:

Father in Heaven, I thank you for loving the world and sending your son Jesus Christ so that I could receive eternal life. I thank you that you have brought me into your house. I thank you for the eternal inheritance that you have prepared for me.

I confess that in some ways I have been looking to receive my reward here on earth. [Tell them to the Father.] I have squandered the inheritance that you intended for eternity. Please forgive me, Father. I choose to come back to your house. I choose to store up my reward for the life to come. I choose to enjoy your presence.

Thank you that you come running towards me now with tears of happiness in your eyes and arms stretched wide open. Thank you that you receive me again as a son. Thank you that you put a ring on my finger, sandals on my feet, and you slaughter the fattened calf for me. Thank you that right now there is a celebration in heaven.

Father, I love you. I love your children. And I love to live in your home.

The Older Son

Think about the older son in Jesus' story. He worked hard to store up an inheritance. But he missed the point – he did not need to earn his Father's love, but simply to enjoy it.

Think about things that you do for the Lord.

- Prayer, worship, studying the bible, attending church meetings
- Your job, ministry in the church, voluntary work
- Serving your family and meeting their needs
- Helping the poor, or other acts of kindness
- Witnessing and evangelism
- Anything else…

Now ask yourself about each one – do you believe that God loves you more because you do them?

Why?

Do you think you will remain in God's favour (his provision, protection, presence, etc) if you stop doing these things?

Why not?

By now, we have begun to see that there is a reward that is linked to our actions. The older son needed to work in order to protect his eternal inheritance. But the presence of the Father and the benefits of his household were not linked to work. They were simply linked to living in the house of God.

The Father loves you unconditionally.

Ask the Holy Spirit to show you any areas in which you have been working to gain the Father's approval. Bring these things to the Father in confession, and thank him for the unconditional love that he wants to pour out upon you today.

Here is an example prayer of confession:

Father in Heaven, I thank you for loving the world and sending your son Jesus Christ so that I could receive eternal life. I thank you that you have brought me into your house. I thank you for your unconditional love towards me day by day.

I confess that in some ways I have been working to gain your approval. [Tell him how.] You have given me an inheritance in heaven, but I have missed the point of my life with you here and now. Please forgive me, Father.

I thank you that I am with you always. I thank you that everything that is yours is also mine. I choose to enjoy your presence, each day of my life.

And when I see someone who has not lived their life with heaven in mind, give me your heart for them too. I want to join in the feast when they return. I want all people everywhere to experience how wonderful your house is.

Father, I love you. I love your children. And I love to live in your home.

Become Aware of Jesus' Presence

Just as Jesus allowed the Father to live through him, so Jesus now lives through us, his church. But what do you think this means in practise? How does Jesus live through you?

Over the next couple of days, become aware of the fact that you are actually carrying the presence of Jesus wherever you go. Imagine him working through you when you are at your work place. Imagine him loving and speaking through you when you are with your family. Ask him to guide your thoughts and to show you what he would like to do through your life.

The more you practise imaging the truth, the easier it becomes to believe it. And as your faith rises, you will genuinely experience Jesus working through you more and more.

Set Your Mind on Things Above

Once again, here are four statements to help you renew your mind. As you speak these out loud each day, they will help to remind you of your place in the Father's house. As we read more about the Father's house, they words will begin to have deeper meaning in your life.

- I live in my Father's house and I am always with him.
- Everything that is his is mine.

- He has prepared an everlasting inheritance for me.
- I love my Father and I love his children.

Action!

Titles in *The Father's Love* Series

01	Father in Heaven. Fathers on earth.	Luke Jeffery
02	Heaven's national anthem.	Luke Jeffery
03	The Father's house.	Luke Jeffery
04	The Father's bosom.	Luke Jeffery
05	Accepted forever.	Luke Jeffery
06	Restoring the Father's love.	Luke Jeffery
07	Treasure in Heaven.	Luke Jeffery
08	Faith, hope and love.	Luke Jeffery

Titles in *Timeless Teaching* Series

01	What do these stones mean?	Joyce Sibpthorpe
02	Motherhood – a piece of cake?	Diana Jeffery
03	A walk with wisdom.	Luke Jeffery
04	Four mountains to climb before you die.	Mark Jeffery
05	Can you hear God?	Joyce Sibpthorpe
06	The Christian guide to jobs and careers.	Charles Humphreys
07	Alive for a purpose.	Kofi Owusu
08	Equipped to heal.	Ian Andrews
09	Diagnosing ills and ailments of relationships.	Adedeji Majekodunmi
10	Pursuing Holiness.	Sam Masamba

All titles available from **www.onwardsandupwards.org**.